LRN

KT-493-414

Renewals
01159 293388
www.bromley.gov.uk/libraries

Please return/renew this item
by the last date shown.
Books may also be renewed by
phone and Internet.

Bromley
THE LONDON BOROUGH
www.bromley.gov.uk

Cather

Rain

Raintree is an imprint of Capstone Global Library Limited, a company incorporated in England and Wales having its registered office at 7 Pilgrim Street, London, EC4V 6LB – Registered company number: 6695582

www.raintreepublishers.co.uk
myorders@raintreepublishers.co.uk

Text © Capstone Global Library Limited 2013
First published in hardback in 2013
Paperback edition first published in 2014
The moral rights of the proprietor have been asserted.

Edited by Daniel Nunn, Rebecca Rissman, and Catherine Veitch
Designed by Cynthia Della-Rovere
Picture research by Ruth Blair
Production by Victoria Fitzgerald
Originated by Capstone Global Library
Printed and bound in China

ISBN 978 1 406 25927 8 (hardback)
17 16 15 14 13
10 9 8 7 6 5 4 3 2 1

ISBN 978 1 406 25934 6 (paperback)
18 17 16 15 14
10 9 8 7 6 5 4 3 2 1

British Library Cataloguing in Publication Data
Veitch, Catherine.
Reptile babies. -- (Animal babies)
597.9'139-dc23
A full catalogue record for this book is available from the British Library.

Acknowledgements
We would like to thank the following for permission to reproduce photographs: Getty Images pp. 7 (Frans Lemmens), 12 (Pete Oxford/Minden Pictures); iStockphoto p. 22 (© Burcin Tuncer); Naturepl pp. 6 (© Barry Mansell), 8 (© Nature Production), 9 (© Visuals Unlimited), 10 (© Visuals Unlimited), 11 (© Hanne & Jens Eriksen), 13 (© Anup Shah), 14 (© Ingo Arndt), 15 (© George McCarthy), 16 (© Tony Phelps), 17 (© Anup Shah), 18 (© Jurgen Freund), 19 (© Konstantin Mikhailov), 20 (© John Cancalosi), 21 (© Tony Phelps), 23 (© Tony Phelps, © Konstantin Mikhailov); Shutterstock pp. title page (© Evgeny Murtola), 4 (© Evgeny Murtola), 5 (© paytai, © Monica Cristale, © idreamphoto, © RUDVI), 22 (© Pongphan.R, © Rich Carey), 23 (© RUDVI).

Front cover photograph of a young Parson's chameleon with its mother, Madagascar reproduced with kind permission of Naturepl (© Ingo Arndt).

We would like to thank Michael Bright for his invaluable help in the preparation of this book.

Contents

What is a reptile?

scales

Reptiles have scaly skin.

snake

lizard

turtle

crocodile

Snakes and lizards are reptiles.
Turtles and crocodiles are reptiles.

How are baby reptiles born?

eggs

Most reptiles lay eggs on land.

This turtle digs a hole in the sand.
She lays her eggs in the hole.

This snake digs a hole in the soil.
She lays her eggs in the soil.

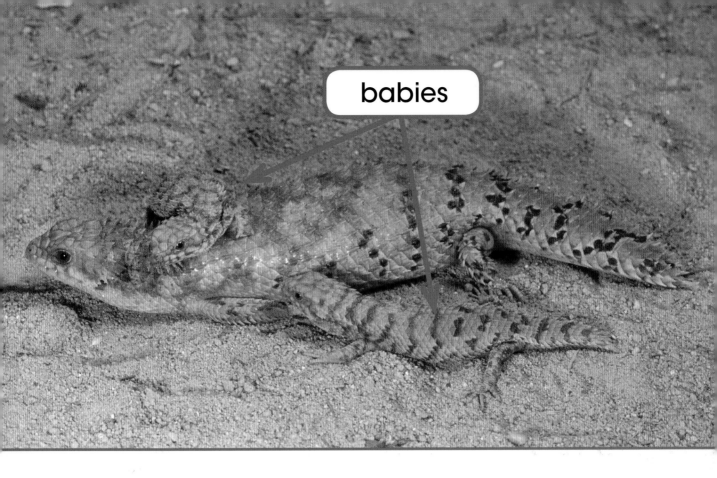

babies

Some reptiles give birth to
live babies.

Caring for eggs

Some reptiles look after their eggs until they hatch.

Many reptiles leave their eggs
in nests.

Hatching

Some reptiles break out of their eggs themselves.

Some reptile parents break the
shells of their babies' eggs.

Most reptile babies look like their parents.

baby turtle

This baby turtle looks like its parents.

Caring for baby reptiles

Some reptiles care for their babies.

baby

This crocodile carries her baby to a safe place.

Growing up

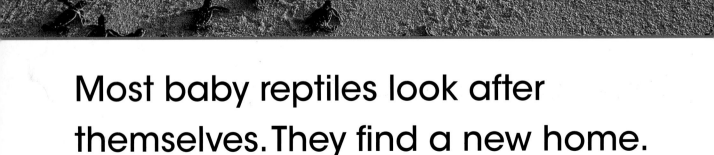

Most baby reptiles look after themselves. They find a new home.

prey

They catch their own prey.

Baby reptiles grow bigger.
They hide from predators.

They find a new mate.

Life cycle of a reptile

egg

adult

baby

A life cycle shows the different stages of an animal's life. This is the life cycle of a turtle.

Picture glossary

 **mate** male or female that an animal has babies with

 **predator** animal that eats other animals

 **prey** animal that is eaten by other animals

Index

Notes for parents and teachers

Before reading

Show children a collection of photos and videos of reptiles. National Geographic and BBC Nature are useful websites. Explain what a reptile is and discuss the characteristics of reptiles.

After reading

- Mount photos of adult and baby reptiles on card, and play games of snap and pairs where the children have to match a baby reptile with its parent. Model the correct pairs first.

- Ask children to label the parts of a reptile: for example, head, feet, tail, scales.

- Look at page 22 and discuss the life cycle stages of a reptile. Mount photos of the egg, baby and adult stages and ask children to put the photos in order. Encourage children to draw a life cycle of a human to compare.

- Compare how different reptiles care for their babies. Discuss the care human babies need.

- To extend children's knowledge, the reptiles are as follows: gecko: p4; skink with eggs: p6; leatherback turtle: p7; tiger snake: p8; skink with young: p9; Burmese python: p10; green turtle: p11; tortoise hatching: p12; Nile crocodile: p13; chameleon adult and baby: p14; freshwater turtle adults and hatchling: p15; adder with baby: p16; Nile crocodile holding hatchling: p17; green turtle hatchlings: p18; hatchling grass snake: p19; spiny lizard: p20; adders courting: p21.